With the new day comes new strength and new thoughts.

—Eleanor Roosevelt

Every day is a new beginning.
Treat it that way. Stay away from what might
have been, and look at what can be.

—MARSHA PETRIE SUE

Keep your face always toward the sunshine—and shadows will fall behind you.

—WALT WHITMAN

I hope you realize that every day is a fresh start for you. That every sunrise is a new chapter in your life waiting to be written.

—Juansen Dizon,
Confessions of a Wallflower

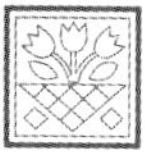

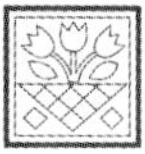

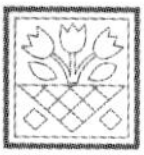

Each day provides its own gifts.

—Marcus Aurelius

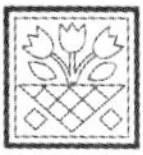

The next morning dawned bright and sweet, like ribbon candy.

—Sarah Addison Allen,
Garden Spells

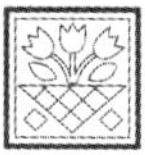

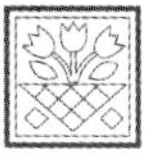

With this morning's sunrise comes a day of things that have never been.

—Toni Sorenson

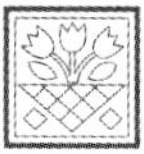

arise full of eagerness and energy, knowing well what achievement lies ahead of me.

—Zane Grey

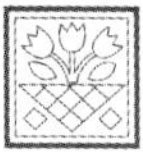

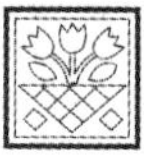